ONCE IN A VERY BLUE MOON

A Pat Alger Songbook

Introduction and Commentary
—— *by Pat Alger* ——

Great Songwriters Series

Creative Manager: Len Handler
Production Manager: Daniel Rosenbaum
Art Direction: Rosemary Cappa
Director Of Music: Mark Phillips

Finale notation was used to engrave
engrave the compositions in this book.

Front Cover collage by Simon Levy
Front Cover photography by Spike
All other photos courtesy of Pat Alger

— • • • • • —

Pat Alger's two albums, *True Love and Other Stories*,
and *Seeds* are available from:

Sugar Hill Records
P.O. Box 4040
Duke Station
Durham, N.C. 27706

Introduction

I am truly blessed to be able to do what I love most—make up songs—and, make a living from it. Whatever success I've achieved is due largely to the great collaborators that I've been fortunate enough to work with and learn from. I am often asked what comes first, the words or music, and except for the rare song I write myself, it's really the collaboration that comes first. I hope you enjoy these songs as much as I enjoyed writing them.

March 1, 1993
Nashville, Tennessee

At Newport Folk Festival, 1969, with fellow writer

The young folksinger, 1969

CONTENTS

With Kevin Welch at a songwriters night in Denver

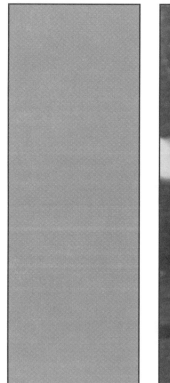

With Richard Leigh at Country Music Association's 1992 "Triple Play Awards"

What She's Doing Now

*Though we're fifteen years apart in age, Garth Brooks and I have a few things in common—one being
we both have an ex-girlfriend in Boulder, Colorado. (Thank God it wasn't the same one.) This
was a very easy song to write and our most successful chart hit—four weeks at No. 1.*

Words and Music by
Pat Alger and Garth Brooks

Goin' Gone

Sometimes when I sing this song, I wonder who wrote it. It's nice to wake up and realize that I'm one of the lucky creators of a contemporary "campfire" song. This one has been sung at several of my friends' weddings—so far they're all still together.

Words and Music by
Pat Alger, Bill Dale
and Fred Koller

Moderately bright, gently

Additional Lyrics

2. From the first time that I saw you
   Standing silent by the shore,
   I knew my search was over,
   And I would look for love no more. *(To Chorus)*

3. There's a ship on the horizon
   Makin' its way against the wind.
   Fom the place where I stand watchin',
   I swear my ship is comin' in. *(To Chorus)*

She Came From Fort Worth

The opening lines, "She came from Fort Worth, but Fort Worth couldn't hold her," are actually about a friend of mine who I had a tremendous crush on at the time. The rest is pure fiction written with Fred Koller.

Words and Music by
Pat Alger and Fred Koller

15

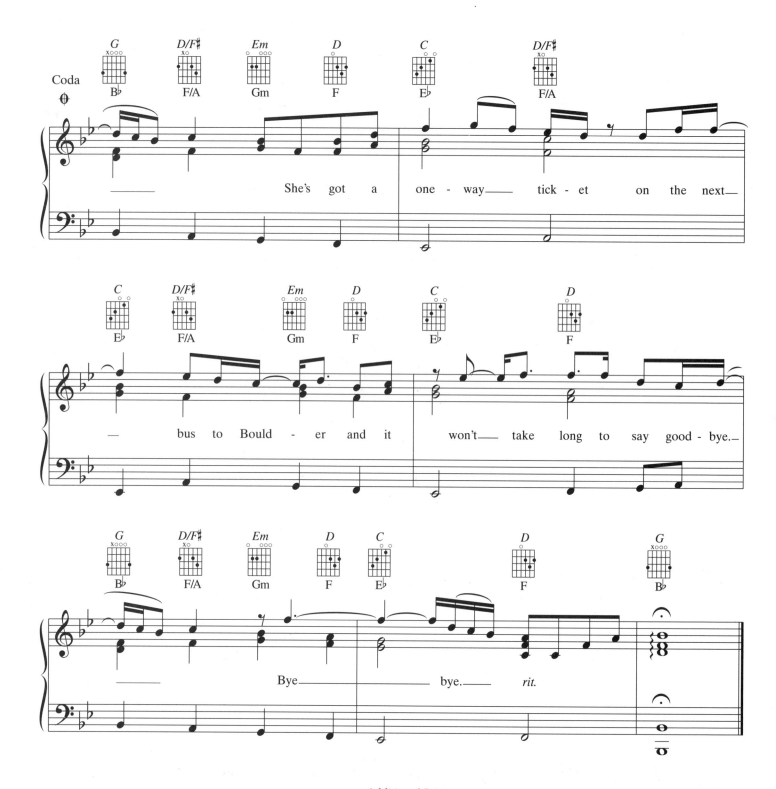

Additional Lyrics

2. And somewhere in the long dark night snow began to fall.
Oh, the world outside was sparkling white when she heard the driver call,
"Everyone off now for Boulder and have a real nice day."
He was waiting on the platform and he raised his hand away.
And she offered no resistance as he took her to his cabin,
And that diner in the distance seemed just like it never happened. *(To Chorus)*

True Love

This was a lot of fun to write and came very quickly. I love to take a familiar idea or title and see if I can write something interesting with it.

Words and Music by
Pat Alger

It's the true love we most— de-sire.—

Additional Lyrics

2. I was alone for so many nights,
   I really started to wonder
   If I had run out of chances to find
   A spell I could fall under.
   Then you walked in like in an Elvis film;
   You were singin' "Love Me Tender."
   I was hypnotized by your blue eyes,
   And the next thing I remember... *(To Chorus)*

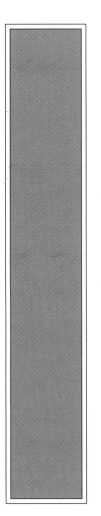

With Larry Bastian and Garth Brooks at the 1991 ASCAP Awards

At the 1991 ASCAP Awards with (l-r) Connie Bradley, Kathy Mattea,
Terrell Ketchum and Jim Rooney

The Thunder Rolls

This was only the second song that I wrote with Garth Brooks. We were trying to write a country "cheating" song that demonstrated the kind of harm that type of behavior causes. There's an extra verse written after the fact, that is the basis for the video version. That verse is included in the live performance video "This Is Garth Brooks."

Words and Music by
Pat Alger and Garth Brooks

wind - shield; there's a storm____ mov - ing in.____

He's head-ing back from some - where____ that he nev - er should____ have been.____

And the thun-der rolls,____

and the thun - der rolls.____

the thun - der rolls. **mp**

To Coda ⊕

D.S. (take 2nd ending) al Coda 𝄋

Coda ⊕   Dm

Repeat and fade

Additional Lyrics

2. Every light is burnin' in a house across town.
   She's pacin' by the telephone in her faded flannel gown,
   Askin' for a miracle, hopin' she's not right,
   Prayin' it's the weather that's kept him out all night.
   And the thunder rolls, and the thunder rolls. *(To Chorus)*

3. She's waitin' by the window when he pulls into the drive.
   She rushes out to hold him, thankful he's alive.
   But on the wind and rain, a strange new perfume blows,
   And the lightnin' flashes in her eyes, and he knows that she knows.
   And the thunder rolls, and the thunder rolls. *(To Chorus)*

Small Town Saturday Night

I was raised in the small town of LaGrange, Georgia, and this song is pretty much the story of my adolescent years. The names have been changed to protect the guilty.

Words and Music by
Pat Alger and Hank DeVito

Bright Country

1. There's an El - vis mov - ie on the mar - quee
2.3. *See additional lyrics*

sign_____ we've all seen at least_

* Recorded a half step lower

dead-end road.____ What's____ the hur-ry son; where're____ you gon-na

go?_____ We're gon-na howl at the moon,

shoot out the light. It's a small town Sat-ur-day night.____ It's a

small town Sat-ur-day night.____

1. D A

Additional Lyrics

2. Lucy's got her lipstick on a little too bright.
Bobby's gettin' drunk and lookin' for a fight.
Liquor on his breath and trouble on his mind.
And Lucy's just a kid along for the ride.

2nd Chorus:
Got a six-pack of beer and a bottle of wine.
Gotta be bad just to have a good time.
They're gonna howl at the moon, shoot out the light.
It's a small town Saturday night.
It's a small town Saturday night.

3. Bobby told Lucy, "The world ain't round.
Drops off sharp at the edge of town.
Lucy, you know the world must be flat,
'Cause when people leave town, they never come back."

3rd Chorus:
They go ninety miles an hour to the city limits sign,
Put the pedal to the metal 'fore they change their mind.
They howl at the moon, shoot out the light.
It's a small town Saturday night. *etc.*

Lone Star State Of Mind

I always loved the idea of a sad lyric with a happy, bouncy melody, and that's what we were going for here. I've had that lonesome feeling many times and this song always pulls me out of it.

Words and Music by
Pat Alger, Fred Koller
and Gene Levine

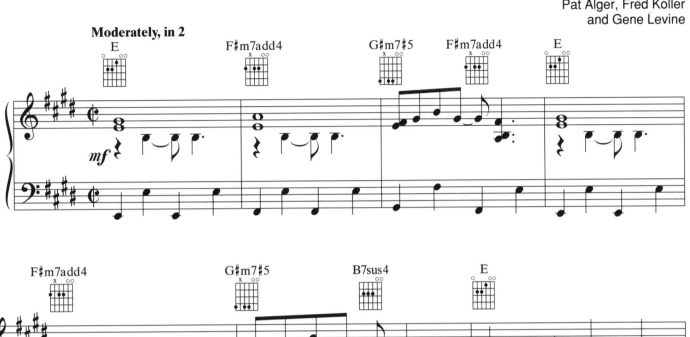

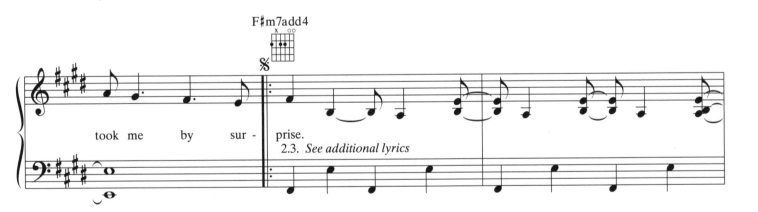

Additional Lyrics

2. Now, Corpus Christi seems so far away,
   I'm not talkin' 'bout the miles.
   There ain't much I wouldn't give today
   Just to see one of your smiles. *(To Chorus)*

3. I just saw John Wayne on the late, late show
   Save the girl and ride away.
   And I was hopin' as the credits rolled,
   He'd make it back to her someday. *(To Chorus)*

Once In A Very Blue Moon

*This is my most recorded song, yet it has never been a bona fide hit record. If I had to pick a favorite,
it would probably be this one because it's as close to a classic as I'll probably ever write.*

Words and Music by
Pat Alger and Gene Levine

Moderate Country

1. I found your let-ter in my
2.3. *See additional lyrics*

mail-box to-day.___ You were just check — ing if I was o-kay.___ And

do I still miss___ you. Well, you know what they say: Just once___

Additional Lyrics

2. No need to tell me you'd like to be friends
   And help me get back on my feet again.
   'Cause if I miss you at all, it's just now and then. *(To Chorus)*

3. 'Cause you act like it never even hurt you at all,
   And I'm the only one gettin' up from the fall.
   Tell me, don't you feel it, can't you recall? *(To Chorus)*

When I dream I dream of this

Pickin' and grinnin' with my twin uncles Leroy and Lamar and cousin Jeremy in Alabama

Stacy Zaferes

Unanswered Prayers

I've probably never been more excited about a song that I collaborated on than "Unanswered Prayers."
I've gotten many letters about this one, because to me it's so universal. Right after it was finished,
Garth Brooks and I sang this at a writer's night, and when we got through the first chorus,
the audience spontaneously burst into applause—we knew we had a good one.

Words and Music by
Pat Alger, Larry Bastian
and Garth Brooks

he does-n't an - swer does-n't mean he don't care.

Some of God's great-est gifts are un - an - swered prayers.

D.S. al Coda

3. She

Lord knows what he's do-in' af - ter all.

And as she walked a - way I

Additional Lyrics

2. She was the one that I wanted for all times,
And each night I'd spend prayin' that God would make her mine.
And if you'd only grant me this wish I wished back then,
I'd never ask for anything again. *(To Chorus)*

3. She wasn't quite the angel
That I remembered in my dreams,
And I could tell the time changed me,
In her eyes too it seemed.
We tried to talk about the old days.
Wasn't much we could recall.
I guess the Lord knows whet he's doin' after all. *etc.*

Somebody's Love

I judged the New Folk Song contest at the Kerrville Folk Festival in 1986, and the winner
was Hal Ketchum. As we got to know each other, I naturally wanted to work with him.
After we wrote this he casually informed me that it was his first co-written song.

Words and Music by
Pat Alger and Hal Ketchum

Seeds

*Both Ralph Murphy and I are avid gardeners, and the idea for this came while Ralph was
planting some Brussels sprouts. I think we harvested a pretty good crop that year.*

Words and Music by
Pat Alger and Ralph Murphy

Moderately fast

times I stop___ on my way home___ to watch the chil - dren play,___
2. *See additional lyrics*

1. Some -

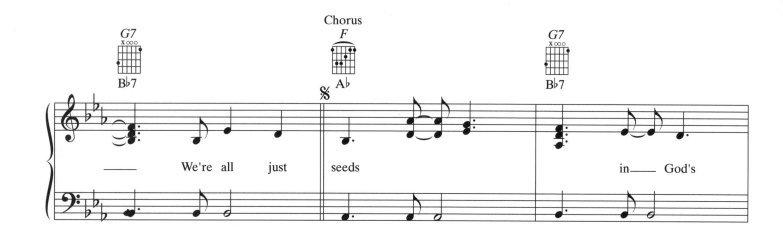

We're all just seeds in God's

hands. We start the same, but where we land

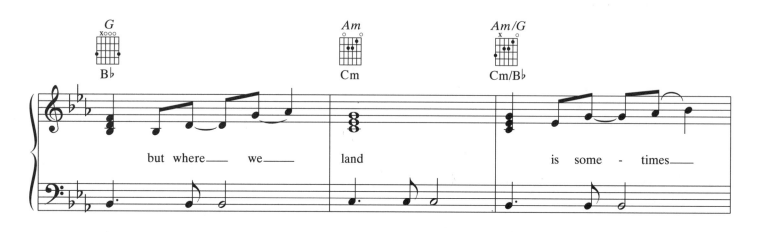

but where we land is some - times

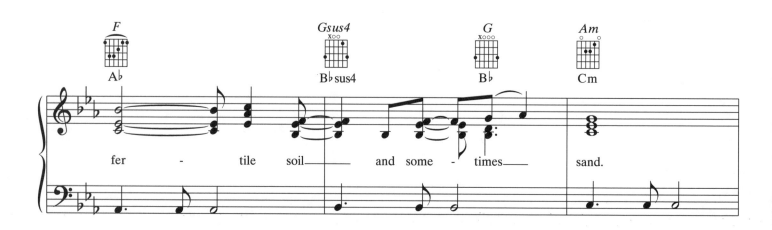

fer - tile soil and some - times sand.

56

Additional Lyrics

2. I saw a friend the other day I hardly recognized;
   He'd done a lot of livin' since I last looked in his eyes.
   And he told his tale of how he'd failed and the lessons he'd been taught,
   But he offered no excuses, and he left me with this thought: *(To Chorus)*

This Town

Probably the best lyric Fred Koller and I ever wrote together was "This Town." It's been
a frustrating song though in one sense—the only people to ever record it have been Fred and I.

Words and Music by
Pat Alger and Fred Koller

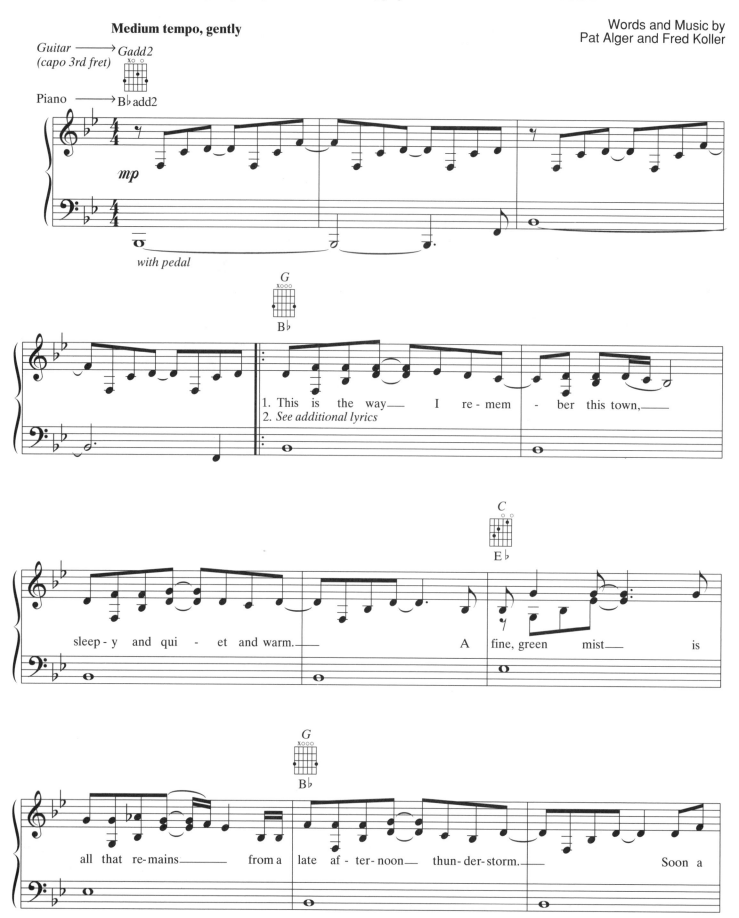

street-light will shine___ on the side - walk___ where a kid left his bike___ in the rain.___

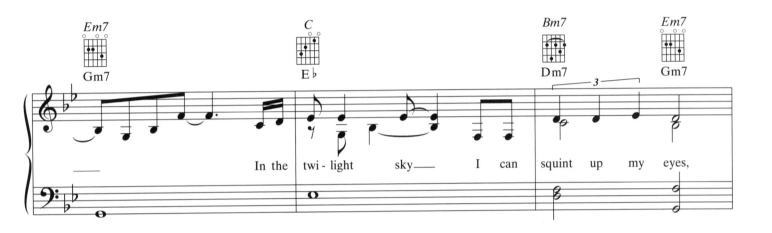

___ In the twi - light sky___ I can squint up my eyes,

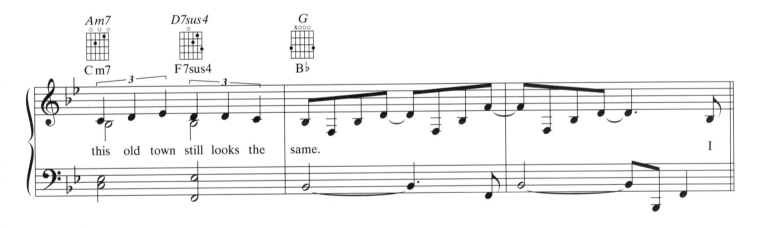

this old town still looks the same. I

Chorus

came to this town___ to re - mem - ber___ some-bod - y I used to

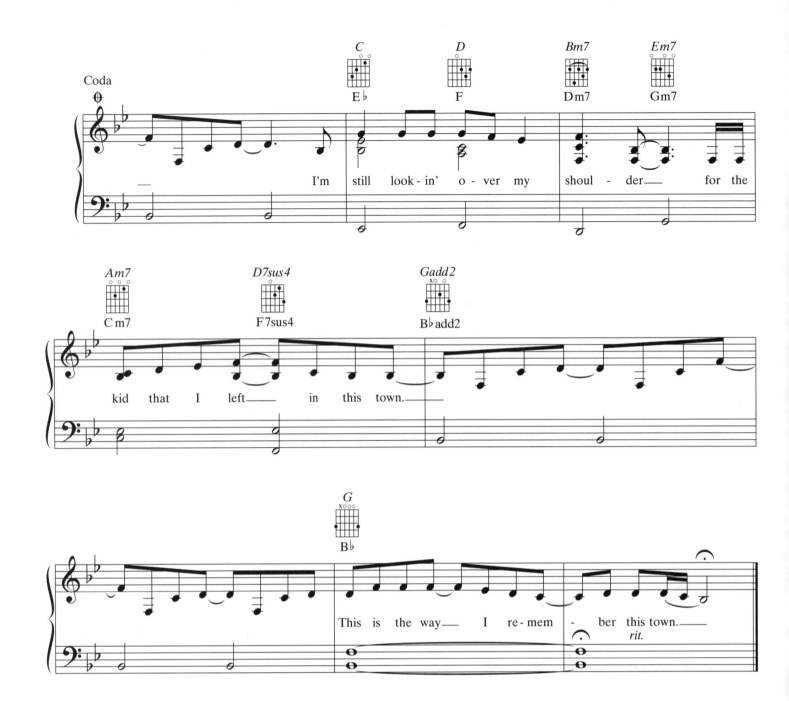

Coda

I'm still look-in' o-ver my shoul-der___ for the kid that I left___ in this town.___

This is the way___ I re-mem - ber this town.___
rit.

Additional Lyrics

2. I'll circle the block, and I'll park 'cross the street
From the house where each Saturday night
We talked about places that I'd never been,
Till your father flashed the hall light.
And sometimes it feels like a long time ago,
And sometimes it's just like yesterday.
And it doesn't take long in this sleepy old town
For me to believe I should stay. *(To Chorus)*

With The Everly Brothers and band on tour, 1992

Angels With One Wing

Richard Leigh is a future Hall of Famer and also one of my best friends.
This is a deceptively simple song that we wrote in my living room while
my friend (and carpenter) Bill was banging away in the next room.

Words and Music by
Pat Alger and Richard Leigh

an - gels with one_____ wing._____ We must

cling_____ to - geth - er to fly._____ We're_____ just_____

an - gels with one_____ wing._____ We must

cling_____ to - geth - er to fly._____

A Few Good Things Remain

I brought the almost finished chorus and the first line of the verse to Jon Vezner one day, and we labored over this song without coming up with anything. He took it with him and about six months later he called me from a phone booth in Minnesota with the completed lyric—great job, Jon!

Words and Music by
Pat Alger and Jon Vezner

Like We Never Had A Broken Heart

*For a year and a half, I was very lucky to have Trisha Yearwood as the background singer
in my band, The Algerians. Her singing this song was always a highlight of our shows.
For some reason, I've always been able to write from a woman's point of view.*

Words and Music by
Pat Alger and Garth Brooks

Like I Used To Do

Tim O'Brien is such a great singer and writer, that I jumped at the chance to work with him.
These lyrics are closer to the way I really am than any other song I can think of.

Words and Music by
Pat Alger and Tim O'Brien

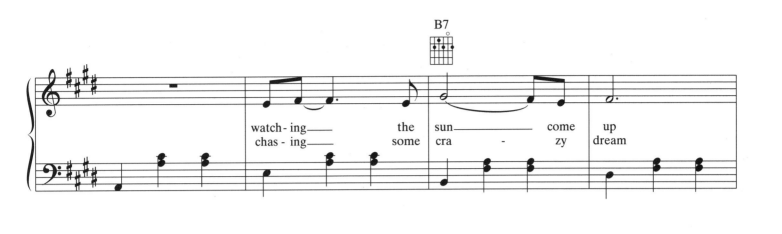

watch - ing —— the sun —— come up
chas - ing —— some cra - zy dream

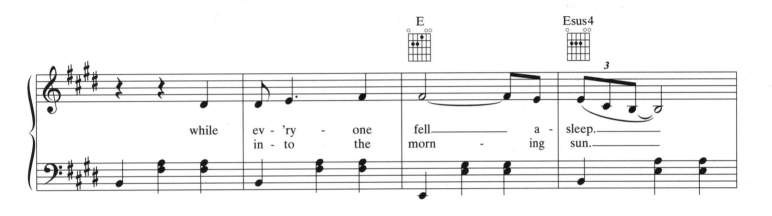

while ev - 'ry - one fell —— a - sleep.
in - to the morn - ing sun. ——

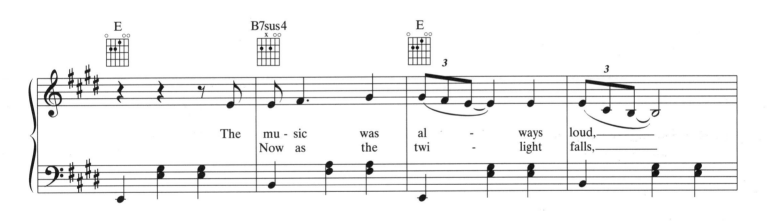

The mu - sic was al - ways loud, ——
Now as was the twi - light falls, ——

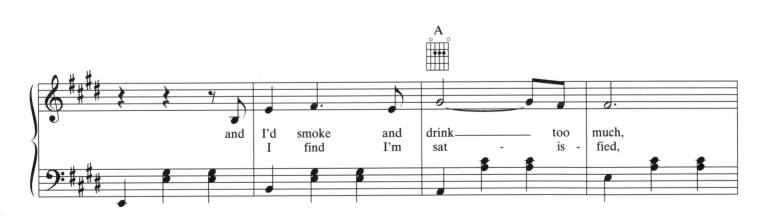

and I'd smoke and drink —— too much,
I find and I'm sat - is - fied,

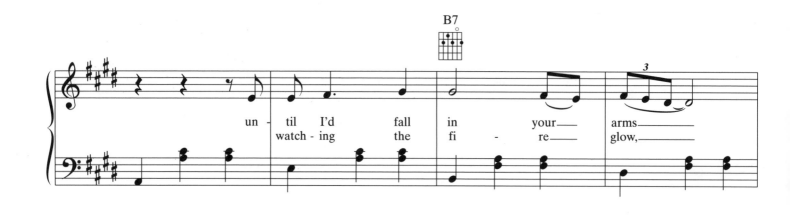

un - til I'd fall in your— arms—
watch - ing the fi - re— glow,—

and in - to your lov - ing touch.—
as long as you're by my side.—

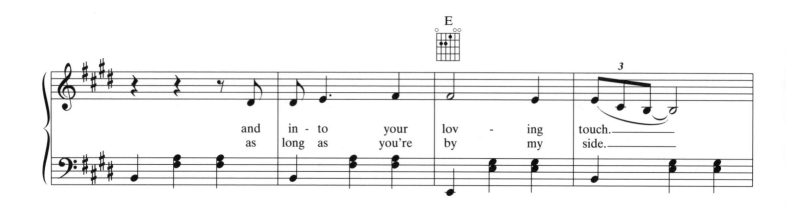

Now as the years roll— by,
Here in my heart it— seems,

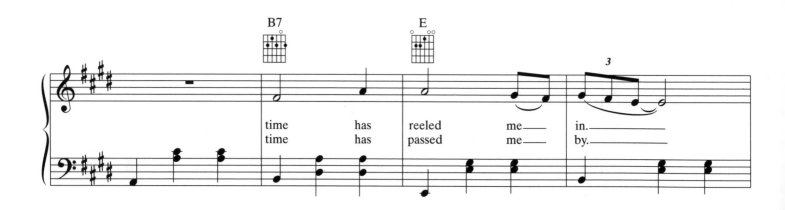

time has reeled me— in.
time has passed me— by.

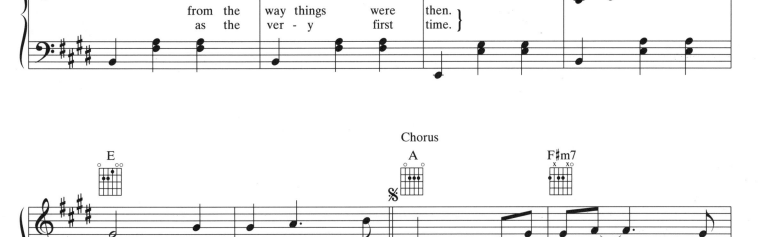

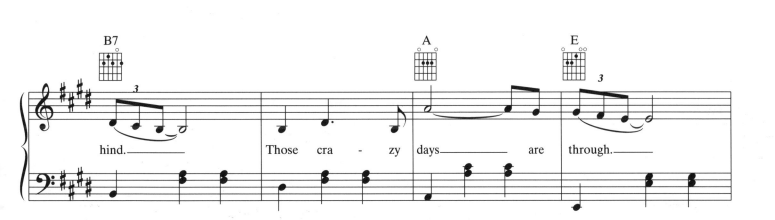

City Lights

Two really great songwriters, Livingston Taylor and James Taylor, paid me an amazing compliment by recording this song. I really enjoy writing story songs about people that I know nothing about.

Words and Music by
Pat Alger

The old folksinger, 1992

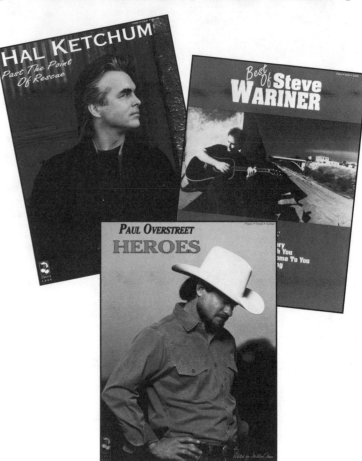